Pearl Rock is the author of *Happiest Moments of My Life*. *Happiest Moments of My Life* is a meditative collection of your innermost thoughts, feelings, and desires. The poems included throughout are striking and inviting. Readers will feel welcome to journey alongside you as you discover your true happiness.

Pearl Rock

LIFE

AUSTIN MACAULEY PUBLISHERS™

LONDON ★ CAMBRIDGE ★ NEW YORK ★ SHARJAH

Ordering Information
Quantity sales: Special discounts are available on quantity purchases by corporations, associations, and others. For details, contact the publisher at the address below.

Publisher's Cataloging-in-Publication data
Rock, Pearl
Life

ISBN 9798891554382 (Paperback)
ISBN 9798891554399 (ePub e-book)

www.austinmacauley.com/us

First Published 2024
Austin Macauley Publishers LLC
40 Wall Street, 33rd Floor, Suite 3302
New York, NY 10005
USA

mail-usa@austinmacauley.com
+1 (646) 5125767

Table of Contents

Time is all we have.

Freedom

The road goes down straight ahead
The streets are restricted inside by square.

The Art of Living

Walking on a field in a crisp morning
Fascinated by the wind, by the rain.

Life Is Like a Movie

Everybody can be a shining protagonist
In your best setting, with your best fellow characters.

Blessing

Each breath, each step
Every opportunity, every meeting
Is this a chance to evolve.

Waiting

Waiting is not a strategy
Yet waiting is sometimes the best we can
Until everything becomes uncluttered
Learning to be patient, and finding a way.

Joy

In the horizon of life and death
You can laugh when you are crying
You can do something stupid when things are serious.

Stubborn Fortress

His reprimand came to be a relief
Letting me take a breath
Tears sinking into black mold
My never-ending thoughts in a storm
Pulling the plug myself
Dialed in to sorrow
Had kept crying bigger and louder
Until my stubborn fortress was tiered down.

Heartless Heart

Shivering under a blanket
That once felt like a cotton feather
And now feels like a crow's wing
Constant delusion made me numb
My auburn heart turning pale
About to terminate the last beat.

Friendly Universe

Every shape and size should be reversed back
If it were a friendly universe
Nothing stays still
In a million pieces of fluidity.

Complete Isolation

A frail cry from one big wolf
Standing alone on an isolated island
But cannot stand anymore
Wanna feel something
The rain running through on the skin
The wind cutting through on the face.

Scared

Starting a day with self-loath
Haunted by bewildering thoughts
Holding on to something that I once let go of
You know how it feels like I have been by myself so long
that I don't know how to ask for help anymore
I am scared.

Indicator

The duty from the universe
The time when everything makes sense
When everything steps off track
The very last indicator.

Wondering Phase

A bunch of hanging words in the air that I cannot reach
The terror of a pause
Used to think the pause is for the best
The courage to put your foot forward.

Tears on a Pillow

A dark and lonely night
A tangled net of emotions run in the veins
Tears overflowing on the face.

Radiating Energy

By the chirping of birds
Growing, blossoming, flourishing
The first window, the new light
The first door, the new air.

Insatiable Desire

23

Deeply embedded soul
Sleeping with the body
The soul was souring high
Floating up in a flash.

Mastermind

24

Thoughts become default
Absolutely no thoughts
Disguise over disguise.

The Invisible

Home is not a place
Love is not a person
Time passes, truth reveals
We say things we don't mean all the time
What's real is behind the façade.

Trust

It is hard to balance out
It is confusing
It's better than being a hypocrite
Nothing is better than having one.

Warmth

Blanket on a bed
Her subtlety of kindness beat me the strongest
The library and stories
A cleared-out room in a quiet.

Just Is

The difference between lost and gone
There is not even a wall and comes indifference
They ask me why
It becomes negative energy.

One

Different view, different being
From the edge of extremeness
Strength of committing to the one
Of letting it go.

Time

Up, down, inside, out
Time of discovery
What you fight for
A way to slow down.

Purpose

Marriage ain't a liability
Family ain't a void filler
For what do you go on.

It Will

To envision the world
Let them imagine
Something gotta give
For something greater.

B.

A car in white
A screen in black
Hemisphere of the white
Covered in floaters
Sphere of the black
Shining stars.

One Flower

An openly closed flower
The floral spirit up to the sunshine
The intangible growth in the stilled stems.

Becoming

It's going, it will get there
The person you becoming vanishes into thin air
A voice on a record, a face in the mirror
Doing the right thing has a way of ending
The person you becoming fast-forwarding
Who deserves more than that
Knows where it's going, and eventually ends
The person who you are
The person who you will be
It's becoming, it's ending.

The Glasses

Last month, the last remains
When given a chance, I did not let go of
For the reason of no money
Its blurs and the invisibles
The style, sophisticated pieces, which differentiates
Messiness from dirtiness
Conventional from traditional.

Mirroring

The age of innocence was maybe the closest to the truth
How do you know what you see is real
If it's told to be real, who will you believe
In the face of the other half, the reflection is mirroring pieces of the identity.

The Day of a Revolution

Having heard as big of a roaring hurricane that could wake us
Jumped into the flood of water, soaking half the body next morning
Is there a 'second chance' after the second chance
Crazy moments can remind of what you were
The number of things that you cannot let go of without fighting it
All I ever remember is humidity inside
Will it ever be clear?

At the Traffic Light

Stopped once out on the road
The chaos where the traffic runs
The road that's reading between the line
Telling us the faintest hint of unspent times
In the flash of moments.

One Step Behind

On the spot, you said so
One who lives by the rules of nature
Chasing ghosts, playing footsteps
Again, the same old feeling that daunts on
The airflow eases little pieces of an entity that conveys us
all
A bitter-sweet energy rushes and hurts you in its aftermath
It's all because you wanted so.

Home

Never realized they were teaching me in disguise
Making fun of me, loving me, spending time together
Like a princess who's somehow living a *normal* life
As though imperfection were perfect
How privileged it was
Coming to the place where you belong.